DREAMSCAPE

Karen Jane Hannington

PublishAmerica
Baltimore

© 2007 by Karen Jane Hannington.
All rights reserved. No part of this book may be reproduced, stored in a retrieval system or transmitted in any form or by any means without the prior written permission of the publishers, except by a reviewer who may quote brief passages in a review to be printed in a newspaper, magazine or journal.

First printing

At the specific preference of the author, PublishAmerica allowed this work to remain exactly as the author intended, verbatim, without editorial input.

ISBN: 1-4241-8665-X
PUBLISHED BY PUBLISHAMERICA, LLLP
www.publishamerica.com
Baltimore

Printed in the United States of America

DEDICATION

This book is dedicated to Benjamin D. Zehner,
the love of my life and my best friend.

ACKNOWLEDGMENTS

My family has always supported me. Without them this book would not have been possible.

Many thanks especially to my friends Carlee Consagra, Jackie and Lenny Elgonitis, Sarah Mehmel, Sue Homm, Jason Hoffman, Doug Mackie, John "Guido" Phillips, Eric Perry, Joe Saltalamacchia, and Ann Marie Alu. In some way, each of them has inspired me to be a better person and to never give up on my dreams.

Gratitude is also given to the following:

Ms. Sally Healey, Luzerne County Community College, English Instructor, for giving me the courage to not only write the words, but to share them with the world.

The entire staff in the Center for Lifelong Learning at King's College for getting me back on track so that I could finally graduate after so many years.

Thanks also go to my former co-workers at Luzerne County Community College in the Academic Affairs Office for always being so kind to me.

INTRODUCTION

It is without question that we all dream. It is something that is as vital to us as breathing. We dream about the moments we wish we could relive and change, the moments we will never forget, and the ones we hope to experience in the future. Regardless of the dream, one thing always remains constant. The dreamer always awakens to a new day full of possibility, wonder, and imagination.

This book of poetry highlights some of those moments that the author experienced in her late twenties and early thirties. From the serious to the more whimsical, each poem has a special place in the author's heart.

These poems can be best summarized by a quote from the poem and subsequent book title *Dreamscape*, whose final line reads, "For what good are dreams to us, if there is no truth in them."

Twilight Time

Twilight arrives slowly.
Casting shadows across the lawn.
Flowers fall into slumber.
Wrapping their leaves and petals
around themselves tightly.
Forming a shelter against the night.
Birds nestle themselves
close to their young.
Keeping them warm and safe.
Bats sound off, silently,
in search of winged prey
abundant now in the
approaching night sky.

Battle Cries

We had a cease fire
in this angry battle
we had been waging.
The peace was over
far too soon.
Long before the ink
had a chance to dry
on the treaty.
There are no more weapons
or armaments left to carry.
All the big guns
have been used up
and cast aside.
My pale banner is raised
in hushed surrender.
Overtake my walls now.
Go ahead, conquer a land
that could have been yours
(without the bloodshed or tears)
long ago.
This time the victory
will be sweet
for only one of us.

Spoiled

I am spoiled
by Cinderella stories
where a lonely girl
dreams herself a prince
or knight in silvery armor.
I am spoiled
by talk shows
where an intelligent host
seems to know something
I do not care about.
I am spoiled
by people I know
who always try to tell me
I am better than they hoped.
I am thankful
for the many friends
who are there to tell me
I haven't been spoiled at all.

Contradiction

I do not believe
in you anymore.
I am weary of your
sweet lies,
bitter truths,
and meaningless words.
You are the Prince
of Contradiction.
I will worship you
no longer.
It is time for me
to find someone
who contradicts you.
Absolution

Absolution

I drown you
in hops
and barley.
Letting the liquid
pardon me
of my sins.
Yet, I know there is
no true absolution.
No safe harbor
from the one
who gets me drunk
on smiles
and kisses alone.

Ali Volat Propriis

She flies with her own wings!
Strong, proud, willful.
Full of her own dreams and desires.
One hand always reaching
for the brightest of all the stars.
One hand always ready
to protect those who are loved.

I fly with my own wings!
Strong, proud, willful.
Testing my strength against the wind.
Unsure, I unfold my wings slowly
offering myself to the sky.
Knowing that all that came before
Has led to this very moment.

Untitled

A little girl sits
silently in the grass
blowing on milkweeds
making wishes
only knowing that tomorrow
she can do the same

A young girl waits
patiently in the hall
looking for acceptance
making plans
knowing that tomorrow
has to be better

A young woman prays
quietly in the church
asking for forgiveness
making amends
knowing that tomorrow
she can be wiser

An old woman rocks
alone in her sadness
asking for an end
making demands
knowing that tomorrow
is too far away.

A Kiss

I had almost given in to
the doubt that lingered
in a heart too tired to fight.
You kissed my doubts aside.
Look into these eyes now
and see the fear hidden deep.
I know that fear plagues you
as much as it does me.
There are reasons to fear it.
There is no black and white.
No one is ever really sure.
We exist in a mist of grey.
It is a leap of faith we take
that leads us down this path.
We can fight our demons.
Together we can have it all.
I don't know where to go,
what words you need me to say,
or what you expect of me.
A kiss like this hangs on,
clings to every cell inside you.
Reminding you of reasons
to be glad to be alive.
I wait with my breath held in
for when you'll kiss me again.
Knowing that it may never come.
Praying that someday it will.

He Sings

I find that I sometimes cannot sleep
When thinking of the things I could not keep
A man's hand that slowly falls away
The words he couldn't bring himself to say
Up there, in false light he proudly stands
Above the outstretched, eager hands
He plays the part he knows too well
Their heaven has become his hell.
I pray he knows of my true heart
Before the song had yet to start
I find myself thinking these things
On the nights, up in lights, he sings.

Darkness Falls

Close your eyes
let the darkness in
feel the warmth
of skin on skin
take yourself
to the place before
the pain took you
to the edge of me
look deep within
the heart of it
and you will see
what pulses through
should never be
the light without
its darker side
a breath away
from serenity
if you could only
let the darkness fall

Absolution

I drown you
in hops
and barley.
Letting the liquid
pardon me
of my sins.
Yet, I know there is
no true absolution.
No safe harbor
from the one
who gets me drunk
on smiles
and kisses alone.

Band of Gold

He took his wedding ring off
as if its absence
would undo the vow he made.
He never knew
the true value of
that band of gold.
I hope he does
someday
for her sake.

As Wishes Fly

She was so full of life
making wishes
on dandelions,
watching them soar,
flying high above the clouds.
To wherever wishes go
in the mind of a child.

Storms

A storm approaches the valley
Dark clouds block out the sun
Turning day into a deep night
Trees bend and sway against the wind
Hoping that their roots are strong enough
To withstand what is about to come
Bright flashes of light pulsate
Accentuating the sky
Large droplets of water
Are thrown violently against the ground
Signs and house creak with pain
As the heaven burst open
Showing nature's true power
Reminding all those below
That nature is all.

Catalyst

You don't seem to smile
    The way you used to
You say that you are happy

You don't crack jokes
    With your characteristic humor
You say things are well

You don't believe in yourself
    The way you always have
You say nothing has changed

You don't smile
As much
You don't laugh
As often
You don't believe
Us when
We say that something is wrong.

You haven't been the same
    As we remember
Since the catalyst came along.

Phoenix

She stares
    carefully
    at me.
Not wanting him
    to catch her.

Making him believe
    in her
    as always.
He used to see things
    even I could not.

He opened my eyes
    only now himself
    is blind.
Blinded by all
    that is her.

As if she burned so brightly,
    That she destroyed all
    with her light.
Even the sun can kill
    Those that get too close.

Words Spoken

I care not
if my words
are meaningless to you.
I need to speak them.
To feel them as
They move across my vocal cords.
Hearing them as they pass my lips.
Though they fall on deaf ears
I will take solace knowing.
I had the courage
To have spoken at all.

Summer

Summer, a little girl,
With bright eyes
And hugs and kisses.
She handles life
Like an Oreo cookie.
Eating all the good stuff
She finds in the middle
She makes us smile
As she wipes the crumbs
from her face with her elbow.
She yells out "I Love You!"
Reminding us what is truly meant
By those three words.

Without

Bees without pollen
Cannot make life-giving honey.
Rivers lacking clear waters
Cannot sustain a larger ocean.
Forests voided of their trees
Cannot offer a safe haven.
A world without peace and morality
Cannot offer our children a future.

Laramie

[Dedicated to Matthew Shephard - 1998]

They tied him to a fence
Beating him and lashing him
They stripped him of his dignity
Robbing him of his possessions
Both real and intangible.
All because this young man
Dared to be different
Dared to be himself.
They left him there to die,
Bloodied and belittled,
And he did.
He did not die alone.
Humanity went there
to die with him.
That part in those of us
who could not accept him
As just a young man.
One that deserved
A better death
if there is one.

You Keep Me

You keep me

Like an old novella
On some bookshelf

Unwanted, Unopened
Though never thrown away.

Are you waiting for me?

You keep me.

As if you hope
I'll still make sense.

How could I?

You never bothered
To pick me up
Off that lonely shelf
To take a close look inside.

False Courage

I was so used to you
Being so brave
Never seeing the coward
Within.

I discovered my true strength
When you revealed
The depth
Of your false courage.

Appearances

I considered your words,
both past and present.
I tried to believe
in your heartfelt attempts at truth.
You told me countless times
that you care for me.
Yet, as you spoke
your eyes lost their glimmer.
your chin dropped.
your brow wrinkled.
Making me wonder
why you held onto me
for so long.
When your countenance
told me
you left a long time ago.

The Visionary

You had lofty goals for me,
didn't you?
You had grand schemes
and even larger dreams
of a life we would have together.
Sorry I disappointed you
with my own ideas
and dreams
and goals
all of my own creation.
With each passing moment
our visions collide.
Blocking any possibility
of becoming one.

The Three Sisters

They each converged together
at different times and places
in the lives they lived.
Over time
these three friends
became more like sisters.
Healing old wounds,
making new memories,
and loving each other
as only true sisters could.

Storm Clouds

There are days now
when I can't help
but doubt myself.
I think of all my mistakes,
misunderstandings,
and misguided beliefs.
They hang overhead
looming like storm clouds.
threatening to burst open
drowning me in penance.
Suddenly the clouds break
A soothing, warm light
radiates from above.
Gently reminding me
of His Eternal love.

Headlights

I looked away for a moment
And you were gone.
With no explanation
you had left my life.
almost as easily as you entered it.
You never thought
I would have noticed
the swiftness of your sudden departure.
The glare of the headlights
through my bedroom window
Weren't so easily hidden
or as easy to dismiss.

Unopened Gifts

There are some gifts
in your lifetime
that will not fit
into any box
to be hidden by
ribbons and bows.

Friendship.
Understanding.
Love.

Theses are the treasures
we should give freely.
For there is precious little time
in which we are able
to give the best of ourselves
to one another.
To do so is paramount
to an unopened gift from God.

Ties That Bind

You have always taken
liberties with me
Expecting to find me
dangling at the end
of the string you taunt me with.

I was always clinging
to the smallest thread
of hope for better things.

Now realizing
the life line had come unraveled.

I have to cut the ties
remaining between us.
I need to set myself free
from the pain I have endured.

Sometimes I am still afraid
hesitant to be the first to let go.

But I know I must release myself
from all the ties that bind me to you.

Ruins

In a moment of anger
a door closed
a friendship lay in ruins
on the stranger's floor
leaving the sole survivor
to contemplate
where the moment had gone
so completely wrong.

The Abyss

I have drifted into an abyss
alone for months
with emotions
running hard and deep.
I am enveloped by
dark, cold waters
in an ocean teeming with life and hope.
I see a warm light
high above me
welcoming me with its gentle glow.
I search for a foot hold
and anchor upon which
to raise myself up
and out of the darkness
into the most beautiful
and loving light ahead.

Late Again

Deep down she knows
his hidden truth.
her intuitions tell her
that his calm demeanor
is nothing more than
a well-worn mask.
He doesn't know that
she saw the lipstick
on his shirt collar
or that she smelled the perfume
that was not her own
when he came into the room,
home late again.
He offered up another excuse
and weak apologies.
Slowly she rolls over
in the bed they share.
She closes her eyes
on the silent wish she made.
Praying that the scent
would leave the room,
and her life,
taking him with is as it goes.

Theatre of Fools

Here is the part in the conversation
that I have dreaded the most.
The act in the play
where one lover tells the other
they can stay no longer
Leaving one to wonder
why it all happened.
The scene is over
the curtain has dropped.
and I am left here
alone
in a theatre of fools.

As I Go

I know these steps I take
have meaning in my life.
Not simply steps to a place I head toward
nor a place I now must leave behind.
They are the moments that make me
change, grow, and believe
that anything is possible.
Please know this…
I take you with me
as I go.

Childlike Prayers

I was only five years old
playing in a graveyard
behind our home in Maine
Sitting amongst the tombs,
dark, grey stones, that marked the lives
that passed long before mine began.

Warm sunshine upon my cheeks
giving promise of a life yet to come.

I would sit beneath
a grand weeping willow
pulling apart milkweeds
letting the seeds blow away
in the gentle summer breeze.

Childlike payers sent forward
to the woman who I would come to be.

Dreamers

I feel in love with you
so easily
so quickly
losing myself to you.
I'd lie in the safety
of your strong embrace
with your heart acting
as the melody
As any dreamer knows
the morning always comes
and dreams are often lost
so easily
so quickly
in the moment before waking.

Levi's

There is a pair of Levi's
we have been whispering about
while sipping on our beers
listening to Van Halen songs
playing loudly on the jukebox.
We consider that life
of that sole pair of jeans
that hugs his body
in all the right places.
He refills our beers
an wonders what
that mutual glance was about.
Never knowing
that he wore the answer.

The Lion and the Tamer

They are the lion and the tamer.
The lion is reckless, passionate.
Waiting for guidance from
someone who will give it purpose
in a world it has never known before.

The tamer is strong, resourceful,
and always in search of a challenge.
Wanting this wild creature
to trust him, meeting him half way.

Looking for the meaning
in their unlikely co-existence.
Forever bound to each other,
two souls defying fate.

Love beyond all reason.
Trust without logic.

A life of love so deeply felt
that nature itself was astounded
by what it had created.

The Last Time

When I came back
you were already gone.
Almost.
You left behind your touch,
you kiss,
and countless questions.
I already knew the answers.
Don't worry
I will be okay,
now.
I hope you know one thing.
You have left me
for the very last time.

Identity Crisis

Grown used to feeling
like less than I really am
Grown tired of always being
the one you let down time and again.
You know no one else
will take this abuse from you.
One day you know me,
the next I am taking up
all your precious space.
My best friend.
My worst enemy.
When you decide which
suits me best
feel free to clue me in.
You will then watch me
as I walk out that door.
As any other stranger would.

Regret

Someone once told me
"No promises, no regrets."
At the time I didn't understand
what he had meant.
Now I know.
You can make promises
on diamonds and gold.
You can envision a life
amongst the brightest of the stars.
Yet, if these vows you make
don't come from
and reside in
the deepest corners of your soul,
then all the wishing
in the night
cannot save you
from a world of regret.

Faceless

Tried not to notice
how you misplace my name
whenever she is in the room.
You called me your friend
but that title was lost to me
now faceless and confused
in a crowded room of strangers.
You only recognize the one
who had broken your heart.
When she is gone
your memory will return
and you will remember who I am.
Will I know the same of you?

Letters

I miss old-fashioned letters
written with pen and paper
in a world of sometimes senseless
emails, faxes, and cell phones.
I long for those times
when I find a simple envelope
awaiting me in the mailbox.
How precious is that moment
when you discover another keepsake
that you can tuck away in a safe place
perhaps for another generation to discover
creating yet another moment,
a mystery within letters.

Good Intentions

Sometimes you make
a wish
with good intentions
learning in time
the intentions
far outweighed your needs.

Speechless

The words cannot
come to me anymore.
You took them with you
when you had left.
How can I express
the anger
the hate
the fear
that you left me with?
I am the candle with no flame,
waiting for someone to show me
the way to forgiveness.
And to light the life
that you stole from me.

The Bartender

He sits alone
on the corner barstool
reading the local paper
just to pass his time.
Sometimes he looks up as someone
walks in for a take-out or quick beer
after their day at work.
Not saying much
he sets about getting what they need
without really thinking much about it.
Once they are gone
he returns to his corner,
back to his crossword puzzle.
Waiting for a better existence
then the one he has now.

Destroyer

I never would have thought
that you,
once my champion,
would be my destroyer.
The one who would
betray me the most.
You saw me though
my worst moments
of my very young life
Through lies,
hardship,
and the pain brought by both.
You were there so often.
Offering a hand to hold,
a shoulder to cry upon.
You built me up so slowly.
Only to shatter me
with one devastating blow.

God's Gifts

How easy it is
to get wrapped up
in the rat race.
We often forget to
do the important things
God asks of us.
Be kind to people we love.
Show respect for others.
Pay attention to each other.
These are the aspects
of human life
that separate us
from God's other creatures.
We are asked to live in the moment
and to cherish one another.
To see each person
that enters your life
for better or worse
and acknowledge the lesson
being taught in it.
Time is so fleeting
making it so easy to miss
these the smallest of God's gifts.

Untitled

Bees without pollen to gather
cannot make life giving honey.
Rivers lacking clear waters
cannot sustain a larger ocean.
Forrest stripped of trees
cannot offer a safe haven to creatures there.
A world without peace and morality
cannot offer our children a future.

Dreamscape

I wonder what I should do with this dream.
It has grown into some other entity of its own making.
So much that this dreamer cannot remember
where the line between truth and fiction was drawn.
I had dreamed of a love that was so strong and deep
that the most forceful currents couldn't wash it away.
The fiercest of earthquakes could never shake it.
The passage of time has no effect on its youthfulness.
I had dreamed of a man who earned my faith.
A man who captured both my flesh and spirit.
A man who encompassed my entire universe.
I loved him for what he was, is, and could be.
I loved him more for what he was in this dream
than for what the real world would ever let him be.
I cared neither for the strength of him arms,
nor did I care for the things he owned or gave me.
The things I treasured most are not physical.
They are intangible, like the truth of love itself.
I loved the way he would stop for no reason
just to glance over his shoulder to look at me
when he thought I wasn't looking in his direction.
I admired his careful approach to children he met.
How he would feel so comfortable and safe to them
that they would tell him their innermost secrets.
I loved the way he would hold my hand as we walked.
How his thumb would trace small, gentle circles
without him being aware he was even doing it.
I was in awe of his spirit for his was unlike any other.
His heart and soul were so well known to me
that I could have written novels on each of them.
His smile would melt away any and all of my sadness
with just a tiny twist of his lips in my direction.
His laughter was infectious and I often fell ill to it.
I would laugh so much and so hard with him that
I would cry tears of overwhelming joy and happiness.

His voice rivaled that of God's most precious angels.
He always knew what to say to ease my troubled mind.
He knew when it was best to not to say anything at all.
Even his eyes had the power to comfort my uneasiness.
He was like seeing the stars shining in the night sky.
Even after the harshest of the summer's storms.
I dreamed of countless conversations between us,
everything from the mundane to the most complex.
I often wondered why a man like this one
would spend his only existence trying to find me,
to seek me out in a world so vast and full of clouds.
I could neither resist him nor deny his existence.
He was as true to me as the sun setting at day's end,
as reliable as the rising of the sun upon a new horizon.
I dreamed of him so often, this man I loved so completely.
Yet, in my morning's waking I could no longer see his smile,
nor could I feel the soothing touch of his thumb on my hand.
I still have faith that I will find this man in this world someday.
For what good are dreams to us, if there is no truth in them.

Manufactured By: RR Donnelley
                     Breinigsville, PA USA
                     August, 2010